PEGASUS ENCYCLOPEDIA
FISH

Edited by: Pallabi B. Tomar, Hitesh Iplani
Managing editor: Tapasi De
Designed by: Vijesh Chahal
Illustrated by: Suman S. Roy, Tanoy Choudhury
by: Vinay Kumar, Sonu, Kiran Kumari & Pradeep Kumar

CONTENTS

What are fish? 3

Characteristics 5

Evolution of fish 10

Adaptations 15

Types of fish 20

What do fish eat? 24

Habitat 25

Relationship with humans 27

Some interesting sea fish 28

Test Your Memory 31

Index 32

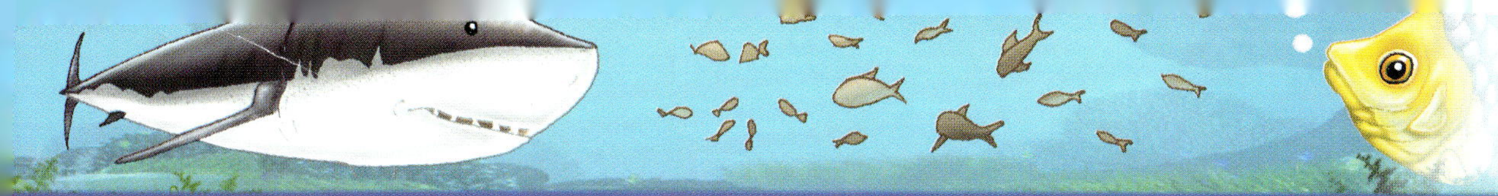

What are fish?

A **fish** is any gill-bearing vertebrate that lives in water and has a skeleton made of either bone or cartilage. Fishes have limbs without digits (fingers and toes). Most fish are **ectothermic** (cold-blooded) which means their body temperatures vary according to the surrounding temperature. Their internal body temperature is, therefore, the same as the surrounding water.

Fish are abundantly found in most bodies of water. They are found in nearly all water environments including streams and lakes located on high mountains to the deepest parts of the oceans.

FISH

There are more species of fish than all the species of amphibians, reptiles, birds and mammals combined. There are about 25,000 known species of fish. More are being discovered everyday. It has been speculated by some scientists that the number might reach up to 40,000!

Fish breathe through **gills**. Gills perform the gas exchange between the water and fish's blood. They allow the fish to breathe the oxygen in the water.

The study of fish is called ichthyology and the scientists who study fish are known as ichthyologists.

Most fish swim using a **tail fin**. Muscles in the tail fin move it from side to side, forcing water backward and propelling the fish forward. Other fins help the fish to change their direction and to stop. **Pectoral fins,** on their side, help them to swim up and down. **Dorsal** and **anal fins** on the top and bottom, keep the fish upright. **Pelvic fins,** on the underside, help the fish steer left and right.

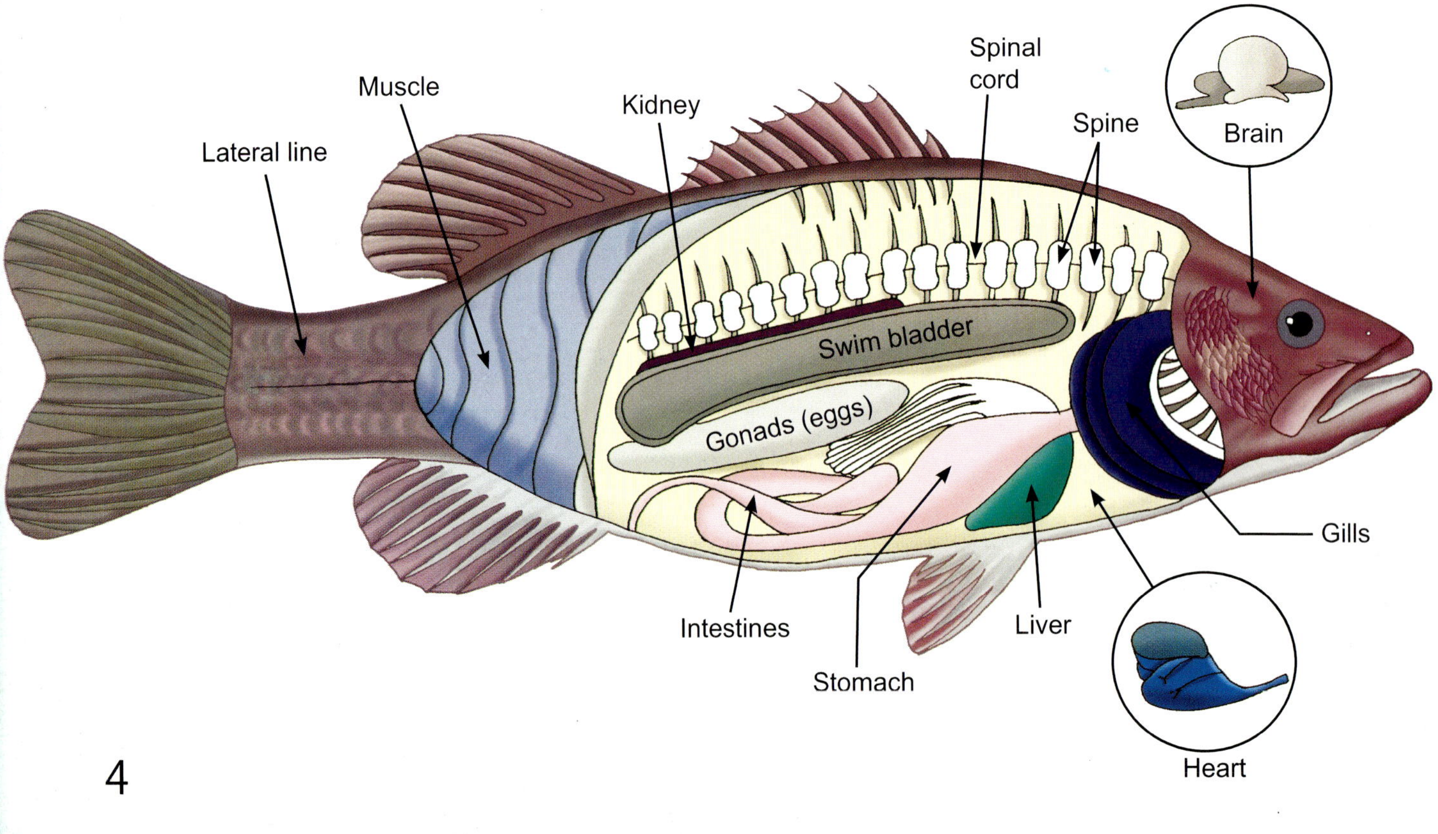

Characteristics

Cat fish

spines in some of their fins that help keep predators at bay. On top of their scales, fish secrete a mucous covering. This mucus is very effective at trapping and immobilizing bacteria and viruses and even contains antibacterial-like agents that will help kill the trapped bacteria. Another important trait of the mucus is to reduce friction and allow the fish to move through the water more easily.

Fish are biologically and behaviourally well suited for living in water. Body shape, feeding adaptations and swimming behaviour are examples of the characteristics unique to fishes.

Skin

The skin of most fish is covered with scales. These scales are firmly attached to the skin and are primarily made of hard calcium. The scales offer protection against injury and infection. Catfish have evolved without scales, but some have hard bony plates and others have sharp

Scales on the skin of a fish

FISH

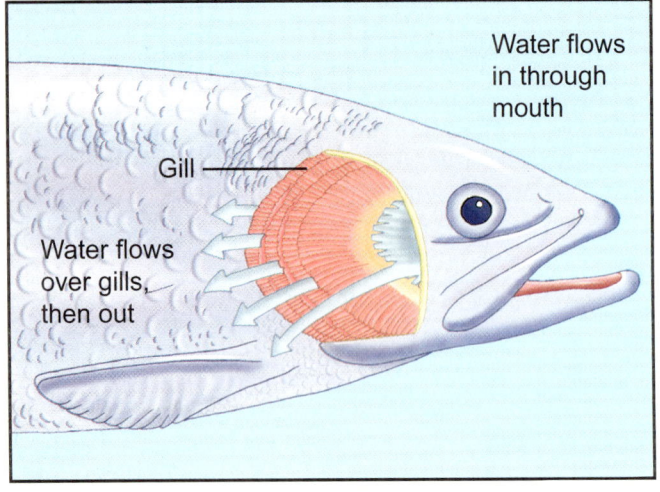
Gills

Respiration

Fish do not have lungs like humans. Fish breathe oxygen dissolved in water with the help of gills located on either side of the pharynx. Gills consist of threadlike structures called **filaments**. Each filament contains a capillary network that provides a large surface area for exchanging oxygen and carbon dioxide. Fish exchange gases by pulling oxygen-rich water through their mouths and pumping it over their gills. Some fish, like sharks and lampreys, possess multiple gill openings. However, most fish have a single gill opening on each side. This opening is hidden beneath a protective bony cover called an **operculum**.

Astonishing fact

The lung fish can live out of water for as long as four years!

Body shape

The shape of a fish's body tells a lot about its lifestyle. Most of the fish have a **fusiform** or streamlined body and are usually fast swimming predators that may swim at high speeds most of the time or are capable of great bursts of speed. A streamlined body is narrow at each end of the body which offers least resistance while swimming.

Characteristics

Many tropical fish are **laterally compressed** that is, flattened from sides. Fish with this shape do not rely on speed for catching food or escaping from predators. Their body shape is very well adapted for hiding in the cracks and crevices of rocks and reef. They can move into these areas to escape predators or to reach a food source that cannot be reached by other fish. Fish with this body shape, such as the angelfish, are capable of short bursts of speed. They are often camouflaged with disruptive coloration.

Some fish are flattened from top to bottom. Fish with such a body shape spend most of their time on the sea floor. They are usually camouflaged or can change their colour to match the colour of the sea floor.

Angel

Fins

Fins are used for swimming and sometimes for protection. The **pectoral** and **pelvic** fins are paired. The unpaired fins are the **dorsal**, **caudal** (tail) and **anal** fins.

Flying fish have wing-like pectoral fins that enable it to glide through the air!

FISH

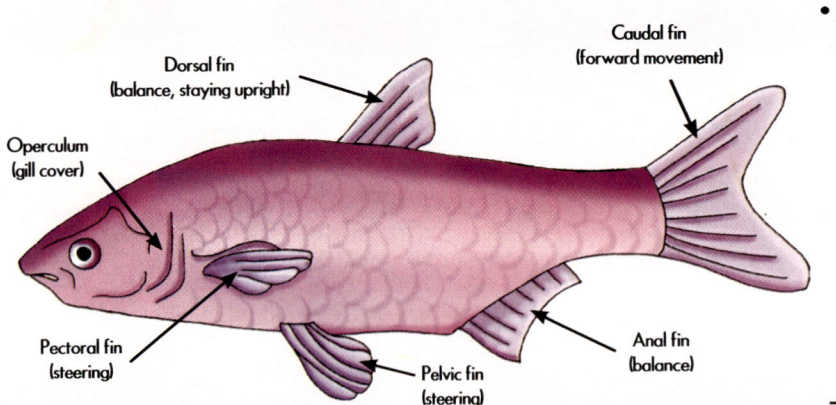

- **Caudal (or tail) fin**: This fin is responsible for propulsion (pushing forward) in most fishes.
- **Anal fin**: The anal fin provides stability to the fish.

Tails

The shape of the tail can be an indicator of how fast a fish usually swims. Fish with crescent-shaped tails are fast swimmers and are constantly on the move. Fish with forked tails are also fast swimmers, though they may not swim fast

The way the fins are used varies among different groups of fish. Most fish use their tails to move through the water and their other fins to steer. Fins of most bony fish are flexible and are supported by visible spines. The shape, location and size of a fish's fins are closely linked to its way of life.

- **Pectoral fins**: Pectoral fins are used for turning while swimming, although they can also be used for other functions such as tasting, touching, support and as a source of power for swimming.

- **Pelvic fins**: Pelvic fins add stability and are used for slowing down speed by some bony fishes.

- **Dorsal fin**: This can be a single fin or be separated into several fins. In most fishes, the dorsal fin is used for sudden direction changes and acts as a keel to keep the fish stable in the water.

Forked tail

all the time. The deeper the fork, the faster the fish can swim. Fish with a rounded or flattened tail are generally slow moving, but are capable of short bursts of speed.

Rounded tail

Characteristics

Eyes

Fish are visual predators. Many fish have large eyes to help them feed in the dark depths of the ocean. Fish such as sharks have pupils that dilate and constrict and some sharks also have an eyelid that closes from the bottom, upward.

Reproduction

Reproduction in fish usually involves laying eggs that are externally fertilized, though a few give birth to live young. Eggs maybe dispersed into the water, laid in nests hollowed out in sea sediments, incubated in the mouth of the adult or attached to rocks or plants in a gelatinous (jelly-like) mass. There maybe no parental care or one or both parents may provide close attention during incubation, hatching and even the first few weeks of life

Evolution of fish

Fish are the first known vertebrates and also the first step to all land-walking vertebrates including human beings. It is now generally accepted that the first vertebrates arose about 550 million years ago.

Agnatha

The first vertebrate that has been found is the Upper Cambrian fossil **Anaspis** which is more than 500 million years old.

These animals, our very distant ancestors, were extremely different to the fish we know today. They were called **Agnatha**, meaning 'without jaws'. There are still some species of fish living today that lack jaws and are, therefore, a part of the Agnatha group.

Being without jaws they had no bones in their mouths and they could not bite. However, they did eat and they had mouths. Among the better known ancient Agnathan fish are the **Ostracoderms** (shell-skinned), so named because of their external armour like skin.

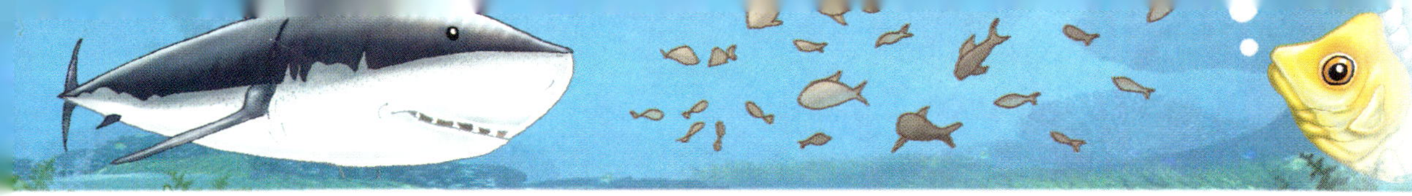

Evolution of fish

The Agnathans lived nearly 360 million years ago in some cases and even until about 210 million years ago.

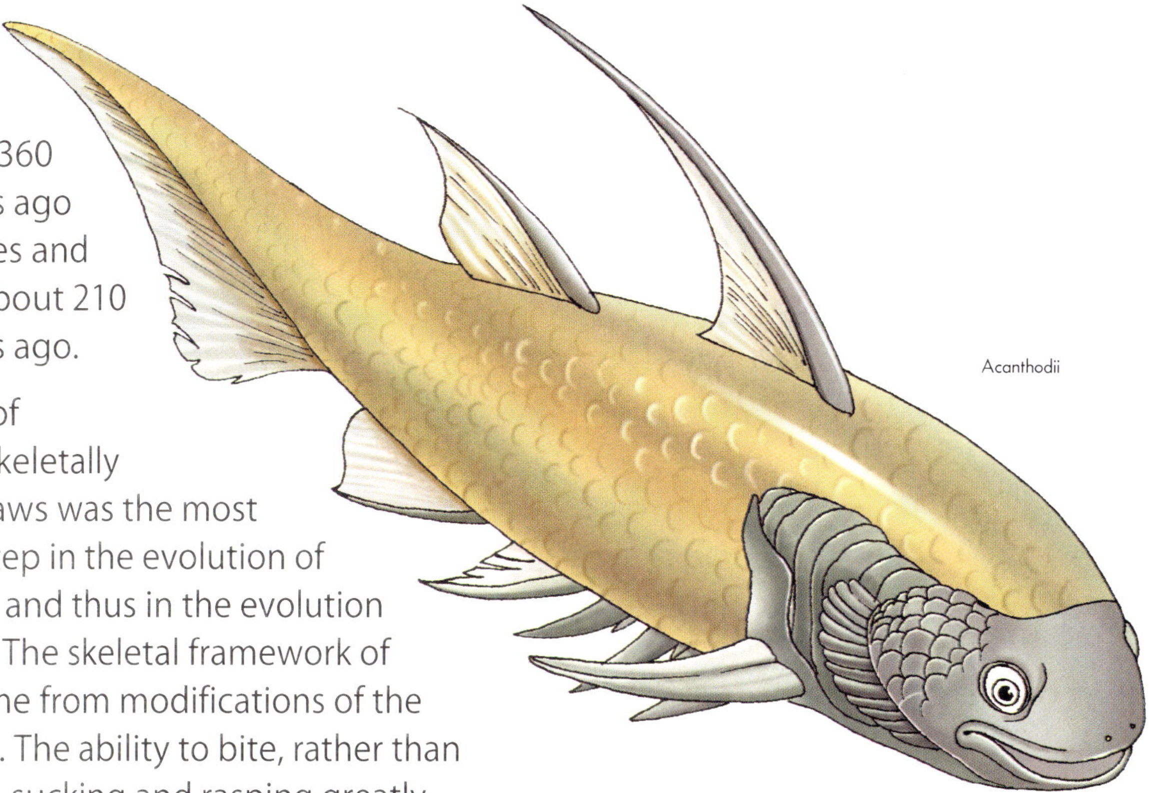

The rise of moveable, skeletally supported jaws was the most important step in the evolution of modern fish and thus in the evolution of mankind. The skeletal framework of the jaws came from modifications of the first gill arch. The ability to bite, rather than just filtering, sucking and rasping greatly increased the fish's range of available foods.

At about the same time as this happened, paired fins, (eventually to become our arms and legs) also evolved. Fins gave the fish lift as it moves forward, an important aspect of the mechanism of swimming.

The earliest jawed fish were called **Placoderms** and **Acanthodii** and they first appeared in the fossil record about 435 million years ago. Placoderm means 'plate skin' and most Placoderms had armour plating, particularly on the head.

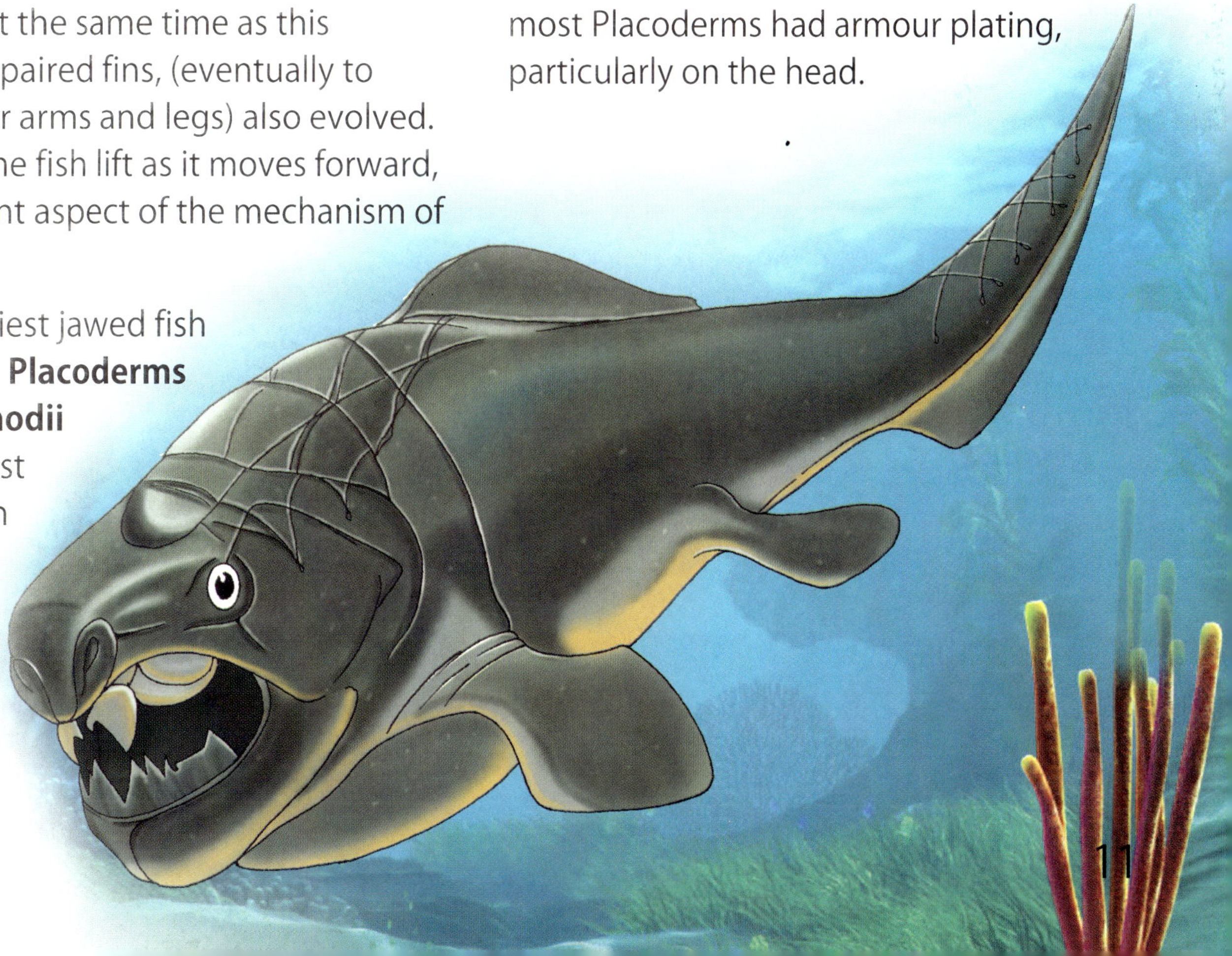

Acanthodii

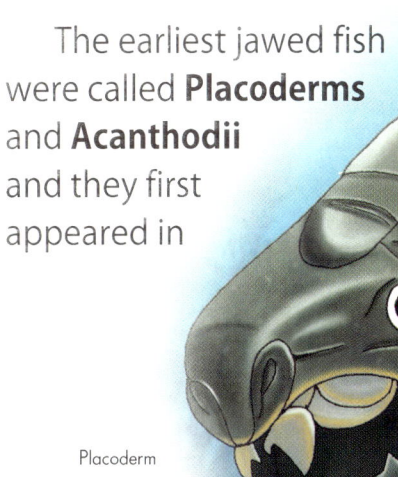

Placoderm

FISH

Arthrodira

Climbing Perch Fish can come out of water in search of food and can also climb trees!

The Placoderms are fascinating not only because they evolved jaws and paired fins, but also because they had the first **swim bladders**. Later on these would eventually become the lungs that would allow vertebrate life to leave the seas and live on land. The Placoderms then had all the essentials to be a very successful group. Scientists recognise about 9 orders of Placoderms, the best known of which are the Arthrodira and the Antiarchi.

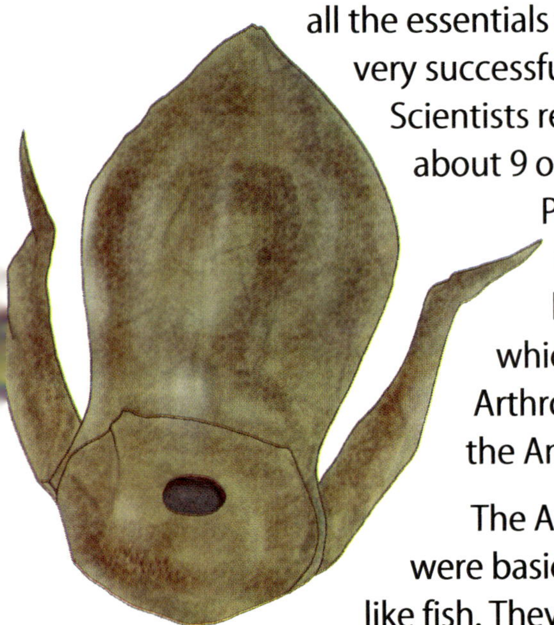

The Acanthodii were basically shark-like fish. They had bony plates but lacked the heavy head armour and this enabled them to move faster. Most species were relatively small as far as we know. They had lateral eyes and large teeth in their jaws as well as dorsal lateral spines. The Acanthodii were successful for much longer than the Placoderms and they remained in the fossil record for 175 million years, upto about 275 million years ago.

Antiarchi

Yellow Perch fish

Evolution of fish

Chondrichthyes

About 20 million years after the first appearance of these two now extinct groups, the ancestors of modern fish come into the fossil record at about 210 million years ago. Both the **Chondrichthyes** and the **Osteichthyes** seem to have evolved from different ancestors at the same time.

The Chondrichthyes are the sharks and rays of the world. Two subclasses of this group are still extant and thrive in our modern waters, only a little changed from their earliest members, which is also the reason why these fish are also known as 'living fossils'.

A third subclass, the **Cladoselarchii**, only appear to have survived for a short while and the fossil record disappeared 15 million years after it started.

The most successful group of fish ever and the group whose members dominate today's water world are the Osteichthyes, the bony fish.

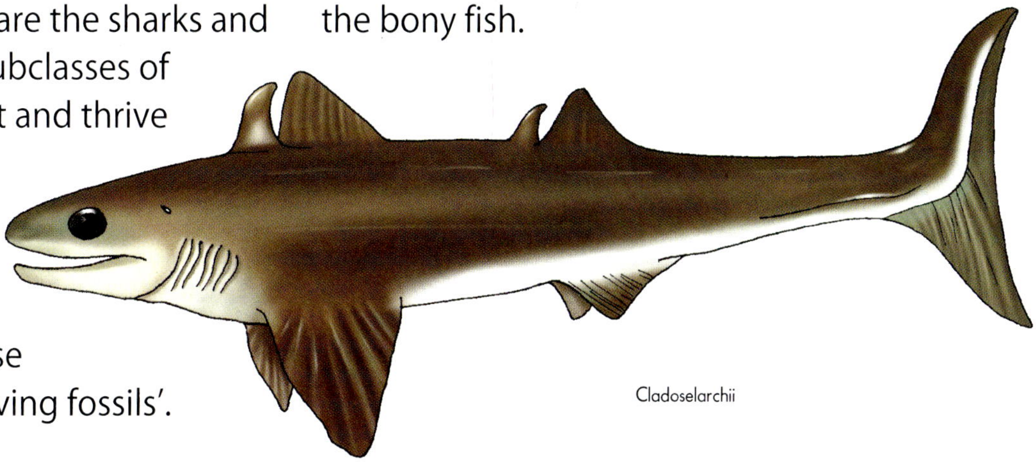

Cladoselarchii

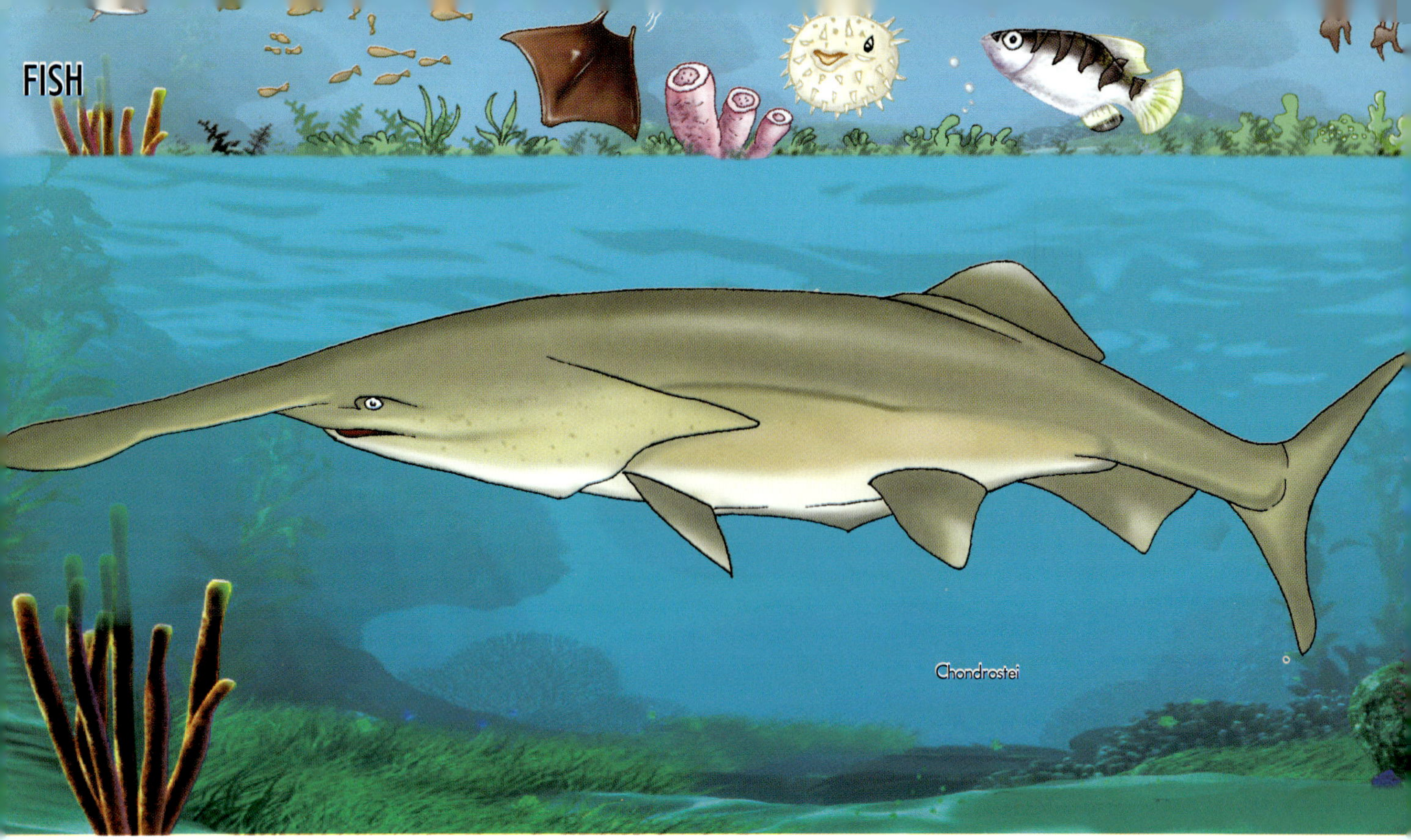

Chondrostei

The first bony fish to appear were the **Chondrostei** (Bichirs, Paddlefishes and Sturgeons) arising about 410 million years ago and they are there still today. After them came the **Dipnoi** (Lungfishes) at about 407 million years ago and then the **Actinistia** (Coelecanths), the **Osteolepiformes** and the **Panderichyida** all around 460 million years ago, the last two of these groups are now extinct.

The majority of modern fish are in the group **Neopterygii**. The Neopterygii are believed to have evolved from an ancestor of the Chondrostei. However, they are late comers in the fossil record appearing only about 250 million years ago. However, since their appearance they have been very successful and most of the fish you see today are in this group.

Neopterygii

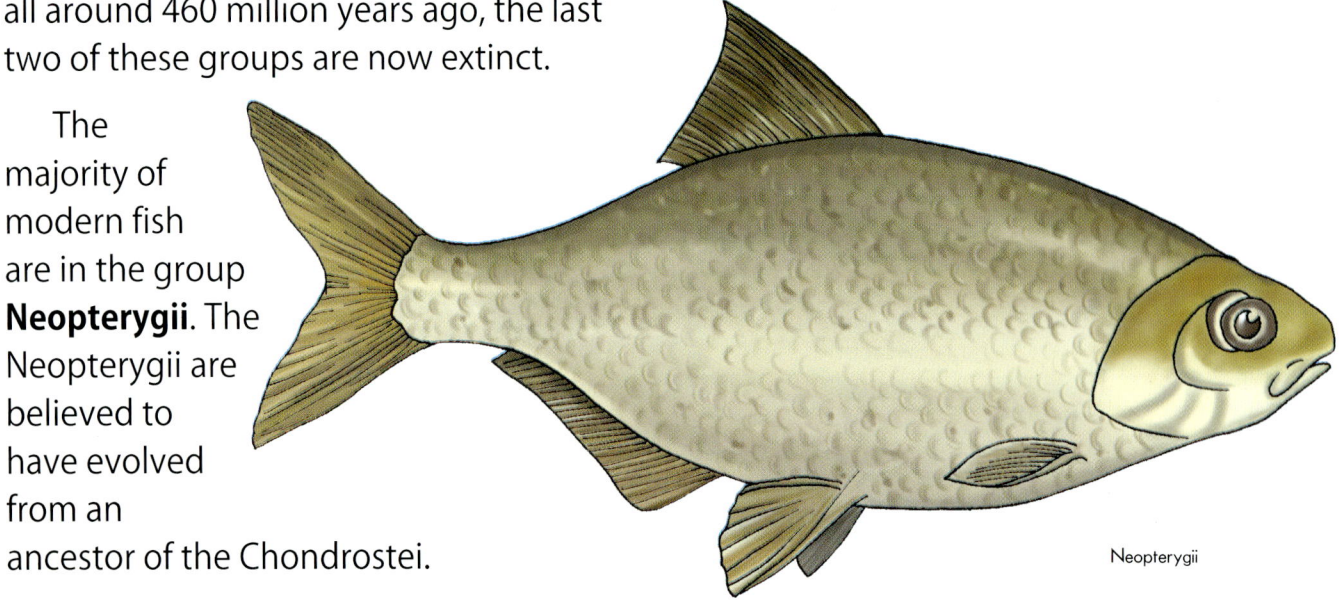

Adaptations

> The Upsidedown catfish from Africa are famous for being the only fish species known to naturally swim, belly-up.

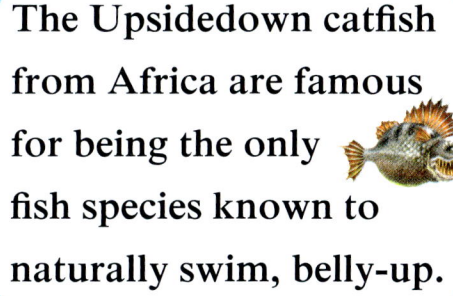

Adaptations

Water is 800 times denser than air. Water also contains less than 2 per cent of the oxygen contained in the air. Sound and light are much distorted in the water. Yet the special adaptations of fishes have allowed them to survive in an environment completely different than that of humans. Some of the common features of adaptation are:

Swim bladder

The swim bladder is a unique organ found only in fish and is sometimes called the 'air bladder'. It is a smooth, gas-filled organ found in the abdomen of most fish. A fish will either add to or decrease the amount of air in the bladder to help it move up or down in the water. Without the air bladder, the fish would have to swim continuously to keep from sinking to the bottom. By adjusting the amount of air in the bladder, the fish can adjust the depth at which they float and extend very little energy in the process. One other benefit of the air bladder in some species is that it can be used to receive or emit sounds.

FISH

Salt regulation

Maintaining the proper level of salt in the fish's body is critical to proper health. The concentration of salt in a freshwater fish is much higher than in the surrounding water. So salt is constantly leaking out of the fish into the water. To compensate for this, fish have developed several solutions. The first and foremost is that they ingest a very large quantity of water

have the same problem in reverse. For saltwater fish, the sea water contains a much higher concentration of salt than what is in their bodies. As a result, salt leaks in and the fish has to use its kidneys to excrete extra salt.

Sight and sound

Most fishes have an excellent sense of sight and can see colours. They have ears but they do not have external openings. The ears pick up vibrations and help the fish in hearing and navigation.

Lateral line

and, as a result, produce a large quantity of urine (10-20 times as much as land mammals).

Their gills too help in extracting salt out of the water and discharges ammonia and other undesirable products. Saltwater fish

Fish also have a unique navigational aid unlike anything found in mammals. The structure is called the **lateral line** and runs along the side of the fish. The lateral line contains small sensory hair that can detect even tiny vibrations. This extra organ allows fish to navigate and hunt prey even in low light or cloudy water conditions.

Adaptations

Colouration

Fish display a wide variety of colours and colour patterns. Skin colouration can have many functions. Many fish have colour patterns that help them blend in with their environment. This may allow the fish to hide from a predator. Some fish, such as the flat fish, can change their skin colouration to match the surrounding habit.

Fish colouration can also be useful in catching prey. Many sharks exhibit colouration known as **counter shading**.

Sharks that have counter shading are dark on the dorsal (upper) side and light on the ventral (lower) side.

With this colour scheme any prey looking down on the shark will see a dark shark against a dark sea bottom, making it hard to detect the shark. Conversely, any prey looking up at the shark, will see the light belly of the shark on the light background of the ocean surface water lit by the sun or moon.

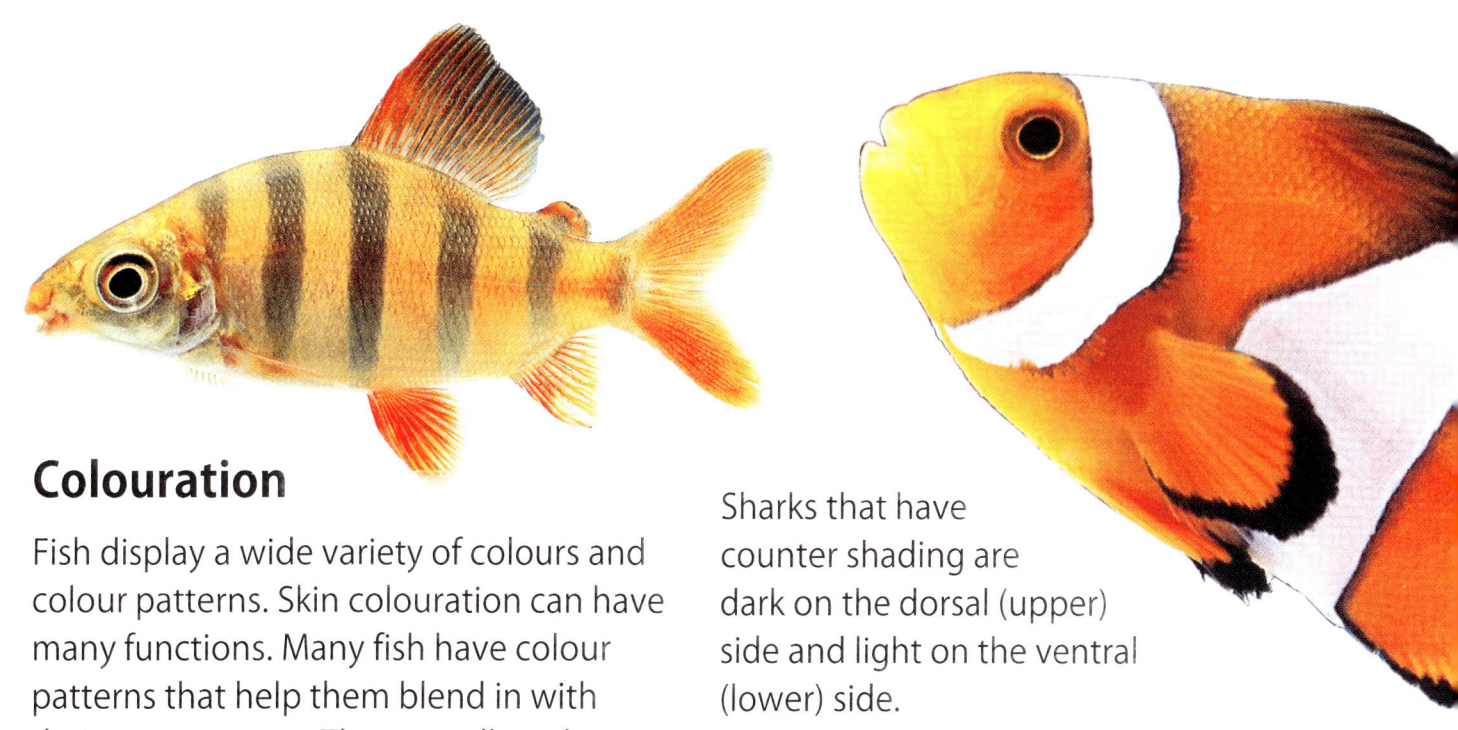

FISH

Young boxfish are shaped like a box!

have spots on their body that resembles eyes. This may serve to confuse prey and predators alike.

Light organs

Some marine fish have the ability to produce light through **bioluminescence**. Most light producing fish live in mid-water or are bottom dwelling deep sea species. In fish, bioluminescence can occur in two different ways, through symbiotic bacteria living on the fish or through self-luminous cells called **photophores**. Some species of Deep Sea Angler fish may use this light to attract prey, while others, like the Atlantic midshipman may use this light to attract mates.

Markings

Fish can also have disruptive markings to hide body parts. Species such as the Jackknife fish high-hat and some Angel fishes have dark lines that run through the eyes. These lines may serve to hide the eyes so that other animals cannot tell where the fish is looking or even if it is a fish or not. Some fishes, like Butterflyfish

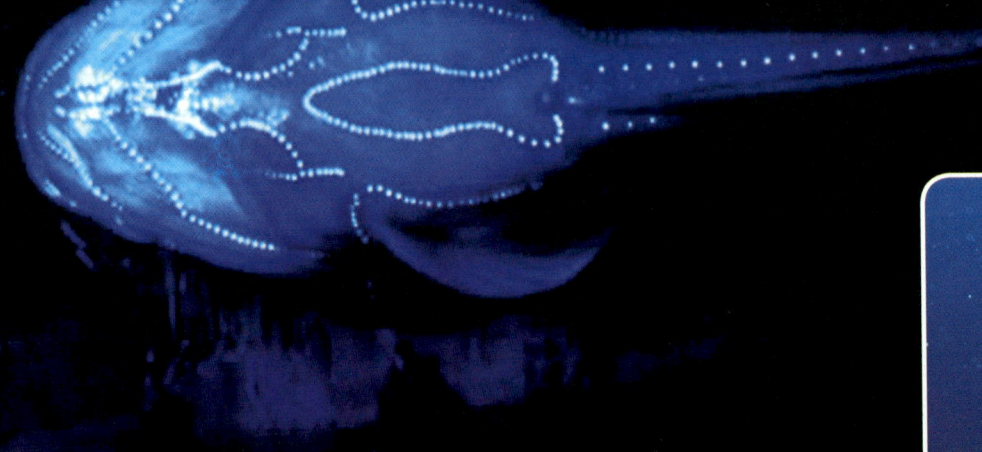

Adaptations

Toadfish

Electric eel

Venom

Many fish may use venom or poison as a form of defence. Most venomous fish deliver the toxins through the use of a spine. Venomous spines are found in a wide variety of fish including stingrays, chimaeras, scorpionfish, catfishes, toadfishes, rabbit fishes and stargazers.

Electric organs

Fish like sharks, skates and rays possess an electric sense system. This system consists of many tiny gel filled canals, positioned on the head of the fish. Through this system these fishes are able to detect the weak electric fields produced by prey.

Some species of skates and rays also have electric current producing organs. The electric rays have paired electric organs located on either side of the head, behind the eyes. With these organs, electric rays are able to shock and stun their prey.

The Electric eel can also produce electric fields. These eels use weak electric fields for navigation, prey location and communication. Additionally, these eels can produce strong electric fields to stun the prey. The strength of the electric current is related to the size of the eel, with larger individuals being able to produce more current.

The Electric eel has an average discharge of 400 volts!

19

Types of fish

According to anatomical structure

Scientifically, modern fishes have been divided into three classes:

- **Agnatha**: The jawless fishes.
- **Chondrichthyes**: Jawed fishes that possess skeletons made of cartilage; and sharks, rays, skates and ratfishes.
- **Osteichthyes**: Jawed fishes that have skeletons made of bone.

Agnathan

Agnathan are also known as the jawless fish. They have no jaw, no scales, no paired fins and no bony skeleton. Their skin is smooth and soft to the touch and they are very flexible. They have a circular tooth mouth by which they bore the body of their victim and suck their blood. Jawless fish inhabit both fresh and salt water environments. Some are anadromous, moving between both fresh and salt water habitats.

There are two major types of Aganthan. They are **Hagfish** and **Lampreys**. The hagfish is the only invertebrate fish and the only animal which has a skull but no vertebral column.

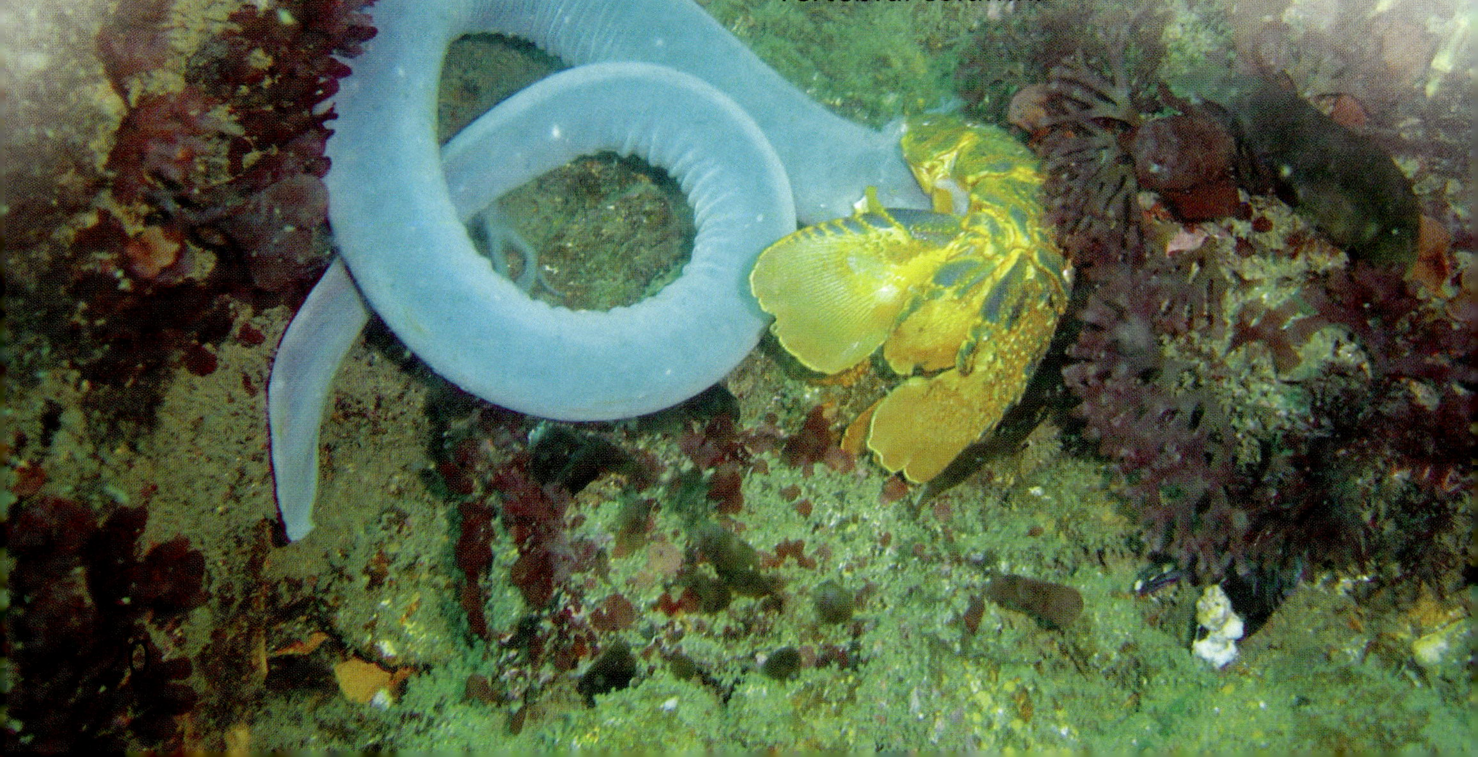

Hagfish

Chrondrichthyes

Chrondrichthyes fish have a cartilaginous skeleton; therefore they are also known as cartilaginous fish. Their ancestors were bony animals and were the first fish to develop paired fins.

The member of the cartilaginous fish possess true bone and also possess a skeleton made up of cartilage. Only the teeth of this species and rarely the vertebrae are calcified. Cartilaginous fish don't have swim bladders.

There are over 980 species of cartilaginous fish. They include sharks, rays and chimaera.

Rayfish

Osteichthyes

Osteichthyes are also known as bony fish. Fishes that belong to this species are spindle shaped, oval and flattened. Skins are protected by protective scales. These bony fishes have a special gas filled chamber called airbladder under the skeleton to allow them to remain floating in water. Another adaptation is **operculum**, a bone on the sides of the fish to protect the chambers that house the gills.

Chimaera

Shark

FISH

Bony fish are again classified into **ray finned** and **lobe finned** fish. Ray finned fish have thin, flexible skeleton rays. Lobe finned fish have muscular fins supported by bones.

The lobe finned fish is the class consisting of lungfish and coelacanths. Ray finned fishes are so-called because they possess **lepidotrichia** or 'fin rays'. Their fins are webs of skin supported by bony or horny spines (rays).

There are three **types of ray finned fishes**— the **chondrosteans**, **holosteans** and **teleosts**. The chondrosteans and holosteans are primitive fish sharing a mixture of characteristics of teleosts and sharks.

According to the type of water

Another basis of division of types of fish is the type of water they inhabit. This division is primarily used for the purpose of keeping fish in aquariums.

Tropical fish live in either salt or freshwater but need a warm (tropical) temperature to live.

Coldwater fish too can live in either salt or freshwater but they need colder water temperatures.

Marine fish live in salty seawater. Usually marine fish need tropical climate.

Freshwater fish live in freshwater and are usually found in inland rivers and streams of most continents.

Rayfinned fish

> **Teleosts are the most advanced or 'modern' fish. They are the dominant class of fish and vertebrates covering about 96 per cent of all extant fish species. They are present in all kinds of water environments from the deep sea to the highest mountain streams.**

Types of fish

Coelacanth

Fish that reproduce in freshwater and have offspring that migrate to the ocean where they spend their adult lives are called **anadromous** (e.g., Atlantic and Pacific salmon). In contrast, fish that reproduce in the ocean and whose young migrate to freshwater to grow into adulthood are known as **Catadromous** (e.g., American and European eels).

According to salinity tolerance

Fish are also categorized according to their **salinity tolerance**. Fish that can tolerate only very narrow ranges of salinity (such freshwater fish as goldfish and such saltwater fish as tuna) are known as **Stenohaline** species. These fish die in waters having a salinity that differs from that in their natural environments.

Flounder

Fish that can tolerate a wide range of salinity at some phase in their lifecycle are called **Euryhaline** species. These fish, which include salmon, eels, red drum, striped bass and flounder, can live or survive in wide ranges of salinity, varying from fresh to brackish (mixed) to marine waters.

23

What do fish eat?

There are thousands of species of fish living in oceans, rivers and other water bodies. It is difficult to classify the food which forms the diet of these fishes. Here is an attempt to make you understand more about their feeding habits.

- **Algae**: The algae forms the diet of herbivorous as well as omnivorous fish. The omnivorous fish eat algae along with the crustaceans for which they actually hunt.

- **Sea grasses and algae**: The fish that eat algae and sea grass are totally herbivorous.

- **Algae and detritus**: Detritus is the coral slime, the solid waste matter released from fishes and the organic matter that gets accumulated over time on the sea floor. This too forms the diet of many fish living at the bottom of the sea floor.

- **Sponges**: Omnivorous fish like the Angel fish feed on sponges.

- **Plankton**: The plankton which includes different types of small fishes, shrimps, copepods, mysids and amphipods which float or drift in water form a supplementary part of the fish diet.

- **Fishes feeding at the ocean bottom**: They survive on any kind of food they get near the bottom of the sea. Their diet includes worms, small fish, crustaceans and almost everything that is edible.

- **Fish feeders**: The fish that eat other fish as prey come under this category.

- **Crustacean feeders**: Shrimps and crabs form the major diet of these fish.

- **Invertebrate feeders**: Small invertebrates that form the diet of these fish are snails, sea urchins, worms and star fishes.

- **Parasite pickers**: Sometimes fish also feed on parasite of other fishes.

Habitat

> Water temperature affects the amount of oxygen that water can hold. Cold water can hold more oxygen molecules than warm water.

Habitat

Fish are found nearly everywhere where there is water with enough food, oxygen and protection. However, not all fish can live in the same kind of waters. Various factors are involved in the selection of a habitat for a particular kind of fish. Take a look at some of them.

Salinity

As discussed earlier, one major factor that separates fish is salt. Some fish cannot live in areas where there is much salt and others need salt in the water to live. However, some fish can live in both saltwater and freshwater.

Oxygen

Even though fish live in water, fish need an adequate supply of oxygen in the water. Living plants within a lake or stream add oxygen to the water through photosynthesis— the process of using sunlight to make food. Oxygen can also enter water from the surrounding air. In a stream, moving water tumbling over rocks picks up oxygen from the air.

Food

The amount and type of food available plays an important role in which fish will be present in a body of water. The amount of competition with other fish is also a factor.

25

FISH

Water temperature

Each fish has a different range of water temperature in which it can survive. Some fish can live in a wide range of temperatures, but some fish require particular water temperature to survive. Although fish cannot always find the exact temperature they prefer, they are usually found in water close to that temperature.

Water quality

Most fish are also sensitive to sediments, pesticides or any other pollutants in the water. Good-quality water will support more species of fish and greater populations of fish than polluted water. Stagnant, polluted or water lacking adequate oxygen will not support large numbers of fish.

Shelter

Fish need places to hide from predators and competitors. They may also need places to rest if there is a strong current. Areas behind rocks, around sunken logs and branches, among patches of vegetation or in deep pools or undercut banks all provide fish with places to escape.

Migration routes

Most fish are very particular about where they will lay their eggs and raise their babies. They will only reproduce if they can find the right type of surface and the right water quality. Therefore, fish often travel a great distance between where they live and eat and where they reproduce. Fish must be able to swim through all the areas in between if they are to be successful in their travels.

Astonishing fact

Desert Pupfish from south-western US and northern Mexico can live in hot springs which can have a temperature of 490° C!

Relationship with humans

Fish as food

Fish is a food of excellent nutritional value, providing high quality protein and a wide variety of vitamins and minerals, including vitamins A and D, phosphorus, magnesium, selenium and iodine in marine fish. Fish, especially saltwater fish, is high in **omega 3** fatty acids, which are very important for a healthy heart and vital to normal brain development in unborn babies and infants. A regular intake of fish is always recommended by most nutritionists.

Fish keeping

Fish keeping is a popular hobby concerned with keeping fish in a home aquarium or garden pond. While most freshwater aquaria are community tanks containing a variety of compatible species, single-species breeding aquaria are also popular. Aquarists also regularly breed many types of catfish, characin and killifish.

Many fish keepers create freshwater **aquascapes** where the focus is on aquatic plants as well as fish. Garden ponds are in some ways similar to freshwater aquaria, but are usually much larger and exposed to open weather.

Goldfish can outlive dogs and cats; they can live up over 20 years!

Some interesting sea fish

Red Lionfish

Red Lionfish is a venomous marine fish found around coral reefs and in the shallow waters of the Indian and western Pacific Oceans. It features a very bright red coloured body. It is as dangerous and predatory as a lion, which is how this fish got its name. One of its spines can cause painful puncture wounds immediately which may last for a week before fully healing. Lionfish grows to 30 cm in length and weighs up to 1 kg. It can move incredibly fast in order to catch its prey. It usually chases crabs, shrimp, molluscs and small fish.

Leafy Seadragon

The Leafy Seadragon is a marine fish and close cousin to the seahorse. It grows up to 45 cm. Leafy seadragons inhabit the shallow tropical and temperate waters of South and West Australia. The protrusions which cover its body resemble leaves and that's how it got its name. Leafy seadragons feed on plankton, algae and water dust.

Long-spined Porcupine fish

The members of the porcupinefish family have evolved an interesting means of defence. When threatened by a predator, they fill their bodies with water until they swell like a balloon. This makes them too large for the predator to swallow. Also, they have pointy spines sticking straight out when it is inflated. If that's not enough of a defence, the porcupine fish's flesh is poisonous to most animals, including humans.

Some interesting sea fish

Stonefish

The Stonefish gets its name from its stone-like appearance. This excellent disguise allows it to blend in with the background as it waits for its prey to wander close enough to gobble. In addition to its gruesome looks, the stonefish has sharp, venomous spines that contain enough poison to kill a man!

Mushroom Scorpionfish

Scorpionfishes are characterized by their bizarre appearance and the numerous spines that cover their bodies. Similar to the lionfish, these spines contain venom strong enough to cause a very painful wound and even more serious injury to those who may have allergic reactions.

Deep Sea Angler fish

The Deep Sea Angler is also known as 'common black devil'. The angler gets its name from the long, modified dorsal spine which is tipped with a light producing organ known as a **photophore**. Like many other deep-water fish, the angler uses this organ like a lure to attract its prey.

A strange fact about the deep sea angler is the fact that the male is smaller and different in appearance from the female. The male of the species is about the size of a finger and has small hook teeth, which it uses to attach itself to the female. Once attached, its blood vessels join with that of the female and it will spend the rest of its life joined to her like a parasite, getting all of its nourishment from her body. If the male is unable to attach to a female, it will eventually die of starvation.

FISH

Archerfishes

Archer fish are unique because of their peculiar way of hunting of insects and other small terrestrial animals from branches hanging above the water. It hunts by firing with great accuracy streams of water into the air to their prey, knocking down animals as big as small lizards onto the water's surface. Once fallen into the water, the fish dashes and gulps its prey. The fish can shoot up to 4 m.

Macropinna Microstoma

Macropinna microstoma is recognized for a highly unusual transparent, fluid-filled dome on its head, through which the lenses of its eyes can be seen. The eyes have a barrel shape and can be rotated to point either forward or straight up, looking through the fish's transparent dome.

The fish normally hangs nearly motionless in the water, at a depth of about 600 m to 800 m using its large fins for stability and with its eyes directed upward. It has been observed that when prey such as small fish and jellyfish are spotted, the eyes rotate like binoculars, facing forward as it turns its body from a horizontal to a vertical position to feed.

Astonishing fact

The males of seahorses, pipefishes, weedy and leafy sea dragons (Syngnathidae family) are the ones that get pregnant instead of the female of the species! This is unique and extreme in the animal world. The females of these fishes insert their ovipositors (like syringes) into a brood pouch on the male's chest and lay their eggs and the male then fertilizes and incubates the eggs. The pregnancies last 2-3 weeks and the male's body feeds the embryos. When the time comes, the daddy gives birth to independent offspring!

Sea horse

Test Your MEMORY

1. What are fish?

2. What is ichthyology and what are scientists who study fish called?

3. With the help of which organ do fish breathe?

4. What is the first vertebrate fossil that has been found?

5. When did vertebrates arise?

6. What does Agnatha mean?

7. Which is the most successful group of fish?

8. What are the three types of fishes according to anatomical structure?

9. What are the types of fishes according to salinity tolerance?

10. Why the Stonefish is called so?

11. What is the other name for Deep Sea Angler fish?

12. What is the name of light producing organ in fish?

Index

A

Agnatha 10, 20
anadromous 20, 23
aquarium 27

B

bioluminescence 18
bony fish 8, 13, 14, 21, 22
brackish 23
breathe 4, 6

C

camouflaged 7
cartilage 3, 20, 21
cartilaginous 21
catadromous 23
cold-blooded 3
coldwater fish 22
colour 7, 17
counter shading 17

E

eggs 9, 26, 30
electric 19
evolution 10, 11
eyes 9, 12, 18, 19, 30

F

fins 4, 5, 7, 8, 11, 12, 21, 22, 30
fossil 10, 11, 12, 13, 14
freshwater fish 16, 22, 23
fusiform 6

G

gills 4, 6, 16, 21

J

jawless 20

L

lakes 3
lateral line 16
lungs 6, 12

M

marine fish 18, 22, 27, 28
migration 26

O

oceans 3, 24, 28
omega 27
operculum 6, 21
Osteichthyes 13, 20, 21
Ostracoderms 10

oxygen 4, 6, 15, 25, 26

P

photophores 18
Placoderms 11, 12
predators 5, 6, 7, 9, 18, 26
protein 27
pupils 9

S

salinity 23, 25
salt 16, 20, 22, 25
saltwater 16, 23, 25, 27
scales 5, 20, 21
species 4, 10, 12, 15, 18, 19, 21, 22, 23, 24, 26, 27, 29, 30
swim bladder 15

T

teleosts 22
tropical fish 7, 22

V

venomous 19, 28, 29
vertebrate 3, 10, 12, 20, 22, 24
vitamins 27